I0425802

This Book Belongs To:

BY
Home Planners And Journals

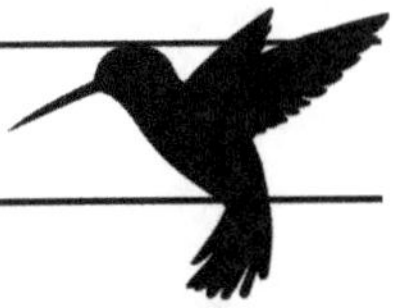

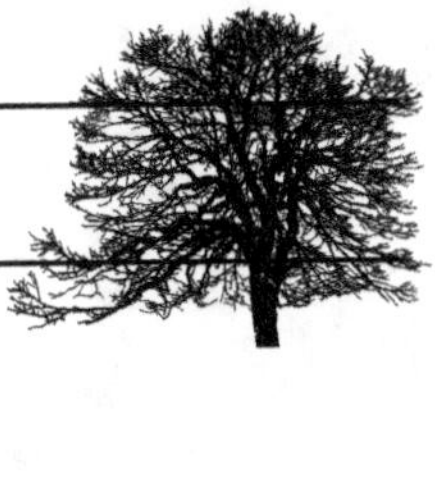

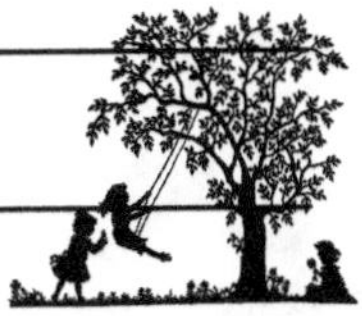

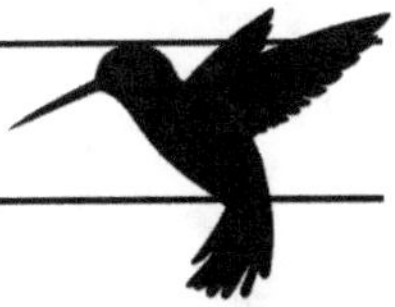

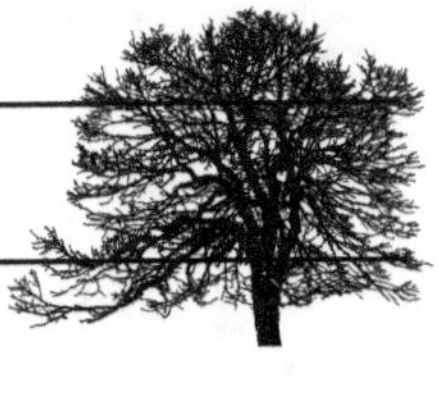

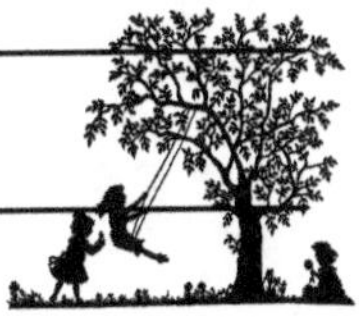

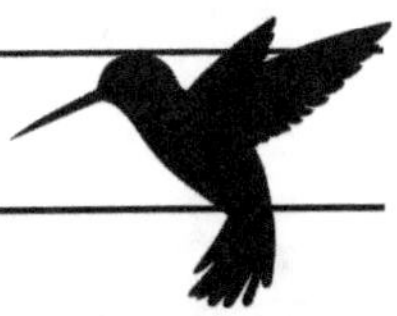

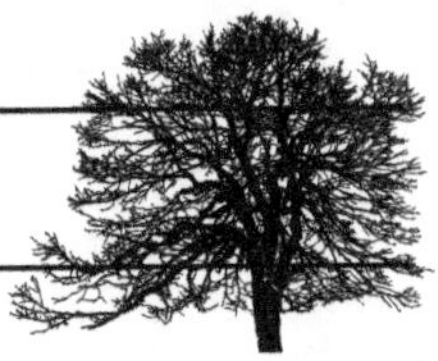

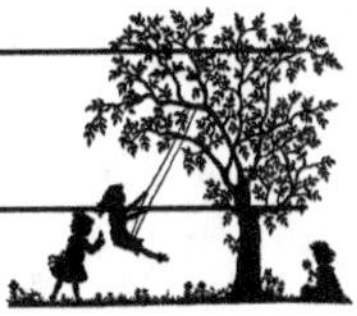

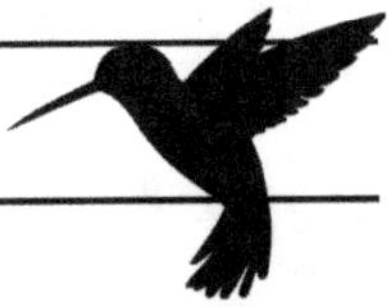

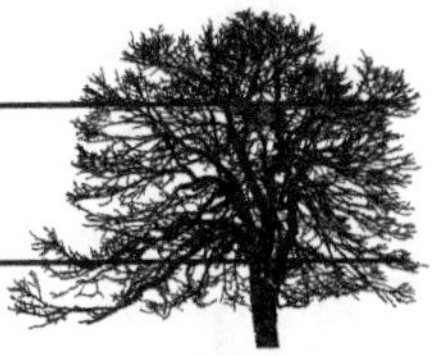

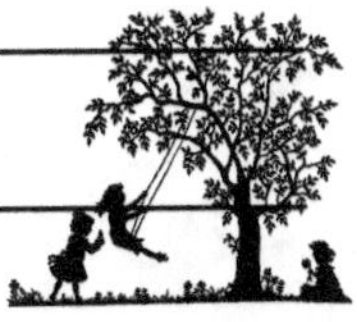

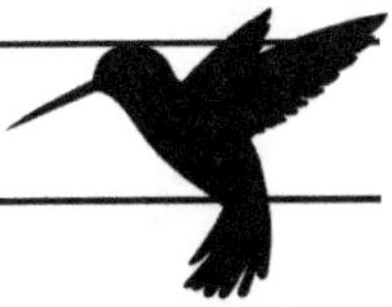

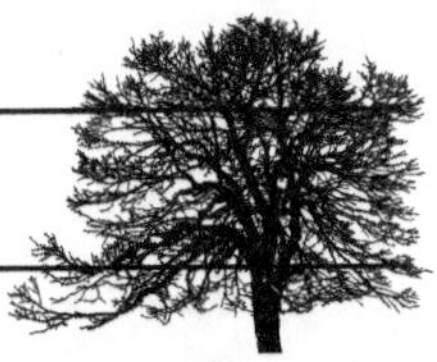

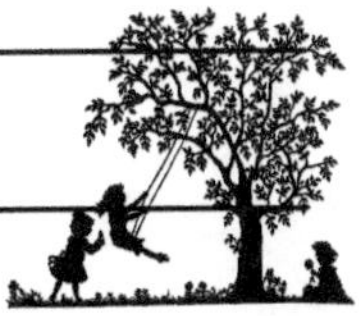

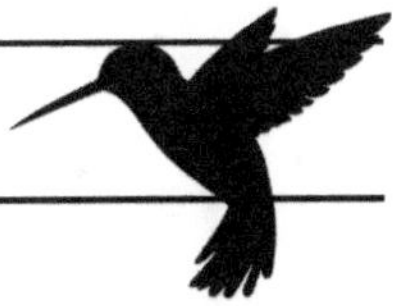

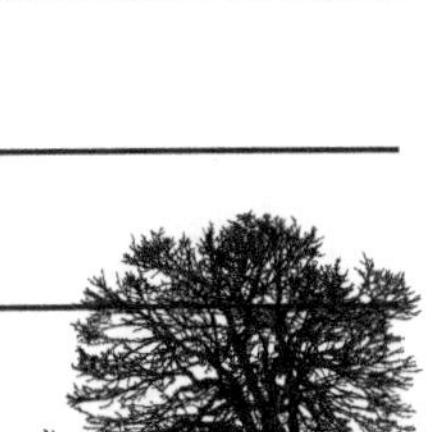

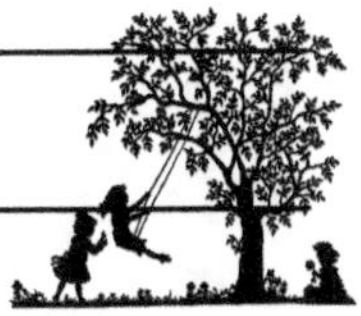

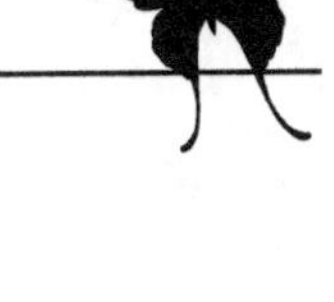

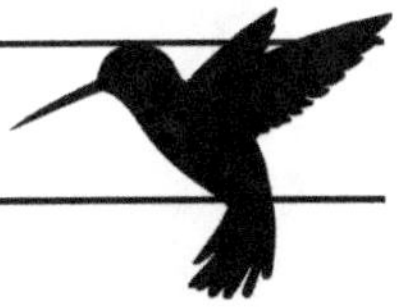

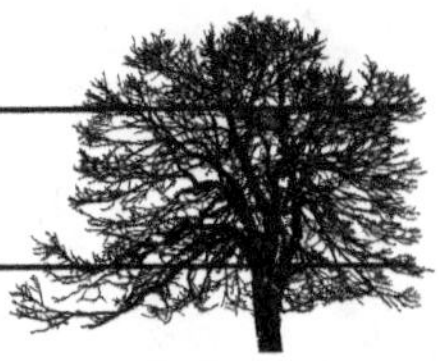

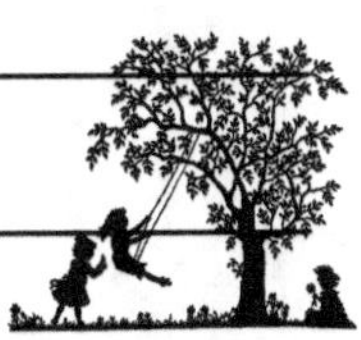

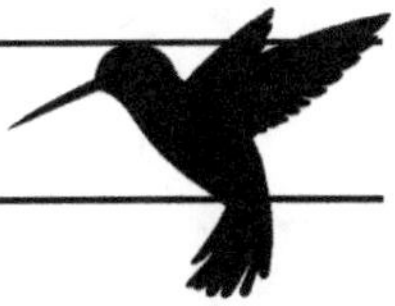

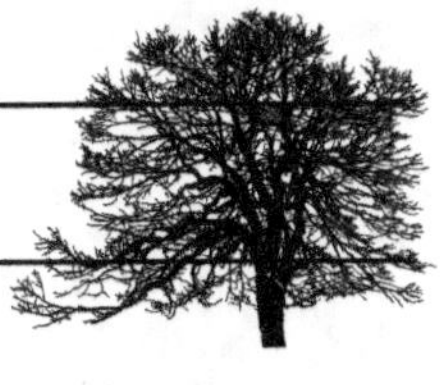

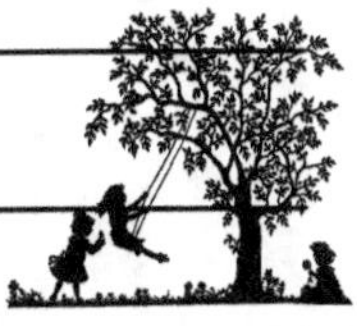

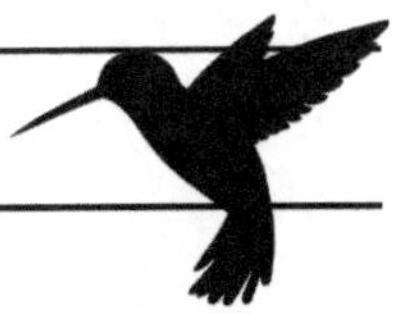

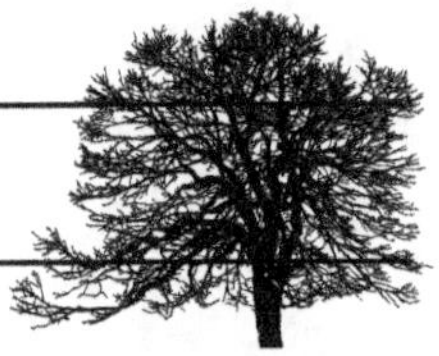

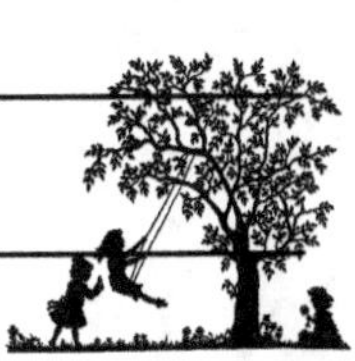

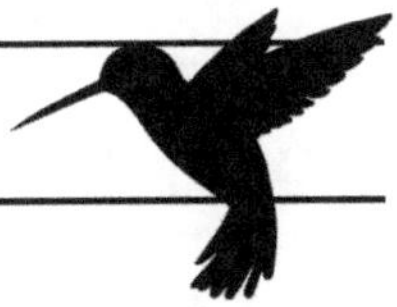

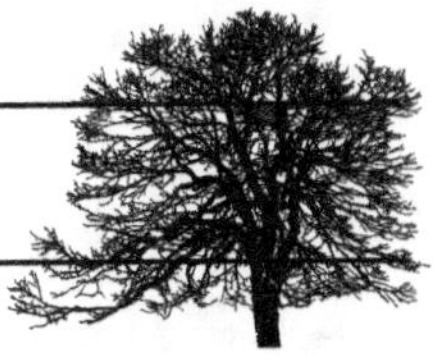

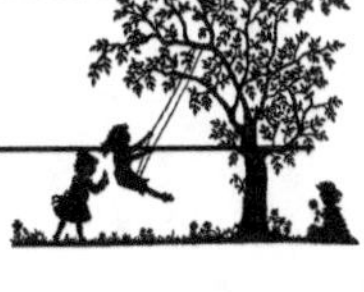

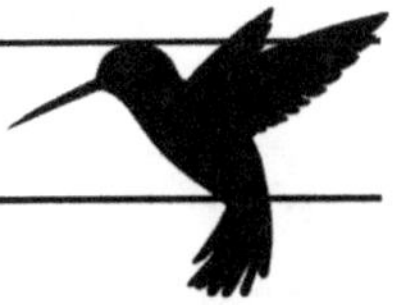

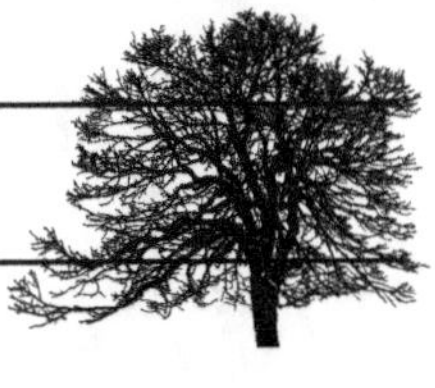

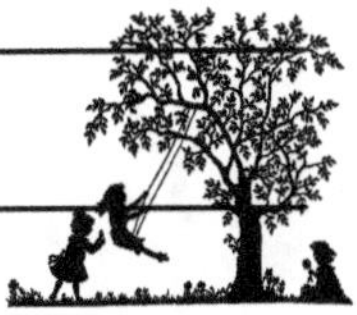

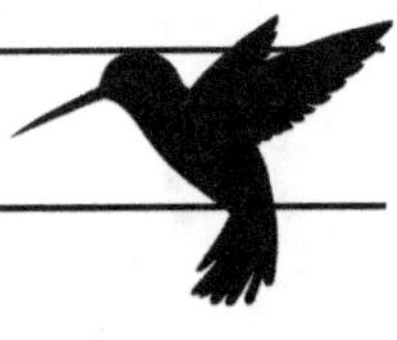

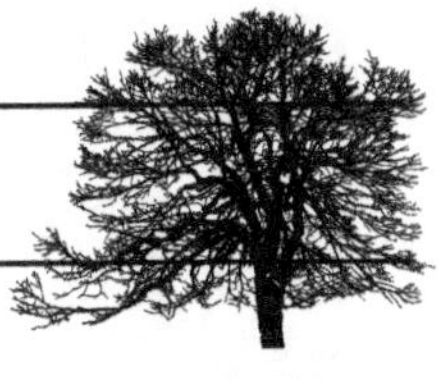

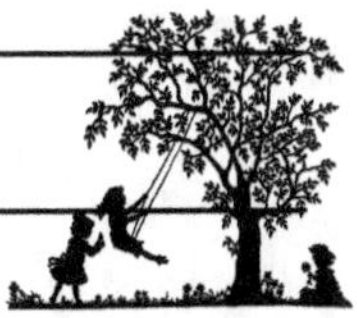

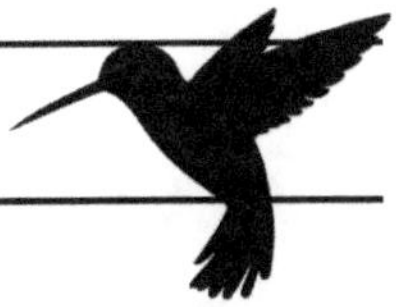

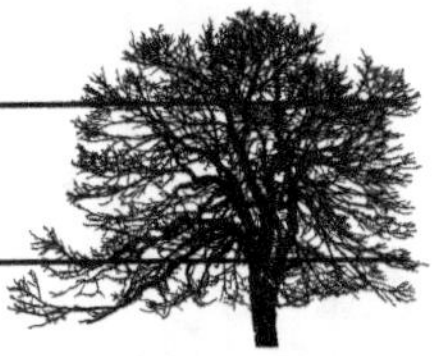

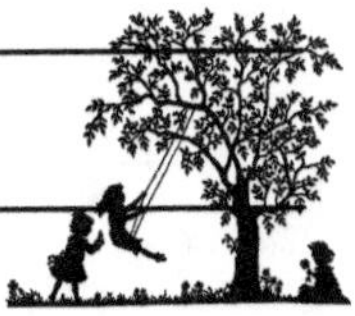

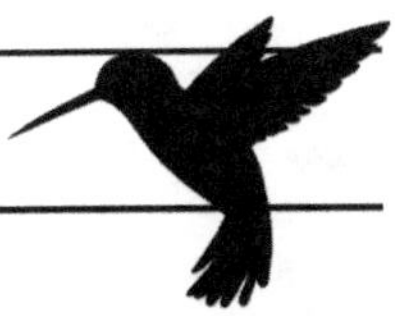

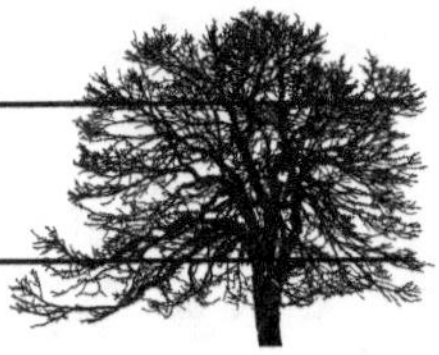

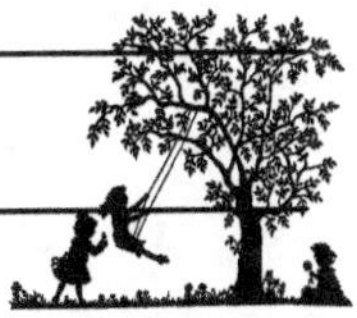

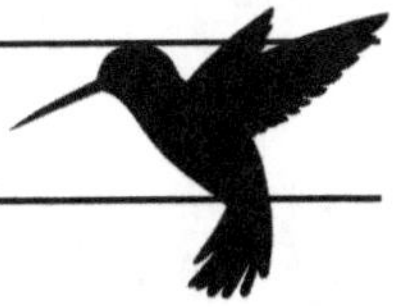

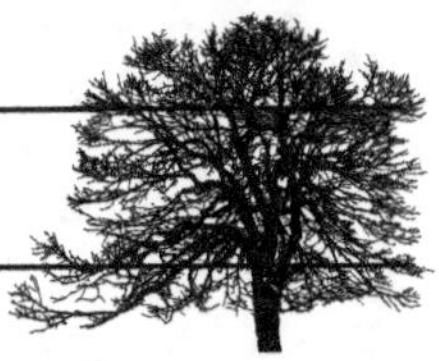

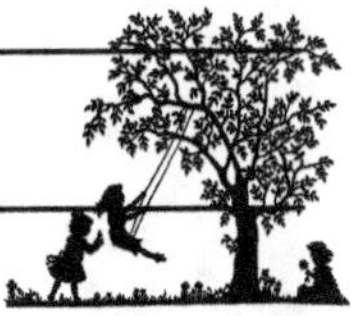

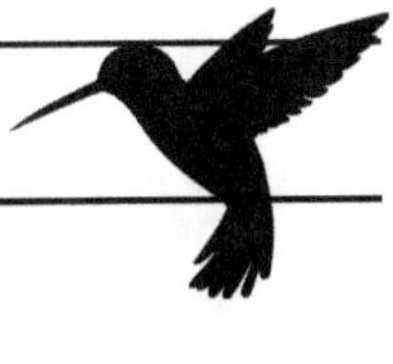

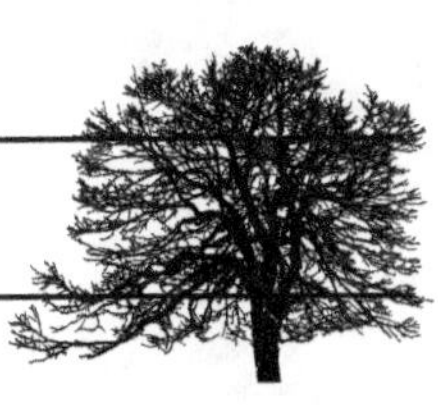

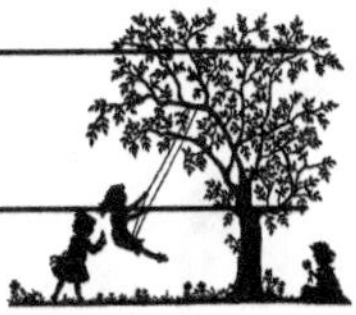

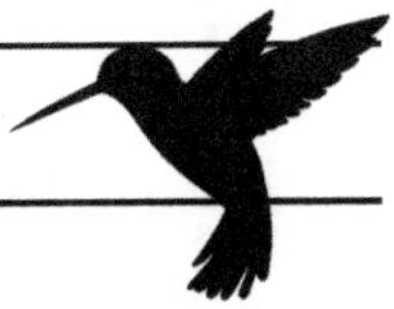

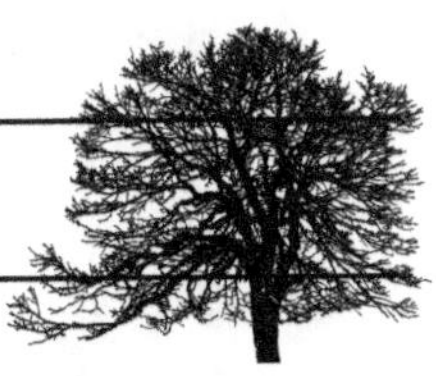

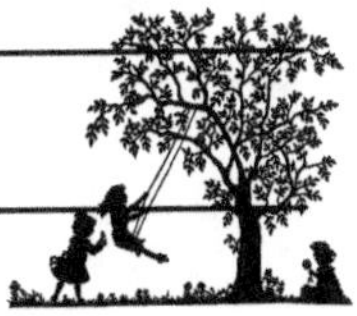

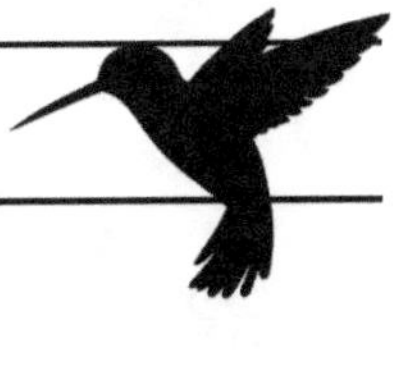

www.ingramcontent.com/pod-product-compliance
Lightning Source LLC
Chambersburg PA
CBHW072051280526
45788CB00006B/2255
9781090216274